द इंडिपेंडेंस

राहुल बी र

Made with ♥ on the Notion Press Platform
www.notionpress.com

क्रम-सूची

क्रम-सूची

क्रम-सूची

INDEPENDENCE DAY

लिखना है आज जरूरी

UNITY

THE INDEPENDENCE DAY

मेरा वतन

Cheluve

प्रस्तावना

"द इंडिपेंडेंस" पुस्तक हमारे देश भारत की भारतीय स्वतंत्रता की सुंदरता को और अधिक बढ़ा देती है, यह हमारे देश भारत के प्रति एक अच्छी छाप और प्रेम पैदा करती है, स्वतंत्रता के क्षण और भी बहुत कुछ। यह हमारे देश के स्वतंत्रता भाग को दर्शाता है। यह पाठकों के प्यार के स्तर और सभी क्षणों में भी बढ़ेगा और सह-लेखकों ने सुंदर व्यक्त, संरचित और प्रस्तुत किया है।

यह पुस्तक "Words Of Soul Publication" के तहत प्रकाशित हुई है और राहुल बी आर "द इंडिपेंडेंस" नामक इस पुस्तक के संकलनकर्ता हैं।

About The Book

The book "THE INDEPENDENCE" upholds the beauty of Indian independence of our country India more over it creates a good impression and love towards our country India, freedom moments much more. It shows the independence part of our country. It will also grow the readers loving level and over all moments and the co-authors have beautiful expressed, structured and presented.

This book is published under "Words Of Soul Publication" and Rahul B R is the compiler of this book called "The Independence".

Gratitude

The completion of this book would not have been possible without the help of my parents, co-authors and friends and also publication too. I thank them whole heartedly for supporting and helping me in every step. So I am dedicating this book of mine to them...

About Publication

Words of Soul is a writing Community and publication where we have a group of new budding writers

with their talent of framing emotions into words.

Formed by Dr. Nikita Dudagi and Lucky pandey on May 15th may 2021 to encourage and appreciate the enthusiastic writers. Weekly Special events and programs are being conducted to recognise the best Writer of the community. Words of Soul a Group of Aspiring writers who inks the emotions of their heart to inspire the reader mind. WOS is India's first ever friendly and best publication. WOS has been registered under MSME. Registration Number: UDYAM-KR-15_0004422

1. ABOUT THE COMPILER

He is Rahul.B.R

He was born on 19/09/1999 Ramanagara district, Karnataka.

But he is perceiving his higher studies in Bangalore. He has completed bachelor degree in science. He like to know more about literature and want to study more and more about it...

He started writing poems from past four years and he writes all kinds of poems... on life, about nature's beauty, love and much more. He is co-authored in many books, Compiler of the book called "The Song

Of Nature", "Nemophilist", "The Song Of Paradise", "Wings To Your Thoughts" and "The Unchosen Bond", "You Are Mine" and few more… and his poems has been published in his college magazine too and he is also english reviewer & community head of words of soul publication.

INDIAN INDEPENDENCE

We got freedom,

With lots of wisdom.

With lots of fight,

More or less late.

Many fought against,

In that there is no doubt.

Finally got independence,

Which was our honest wish.

Now it's our 75 Indian independence day,

So let's celebrate in particular way.

Come let's join together,

With no more far...

2. KEERTHI PRIYA M

Keerthi is a passionate writer. Apart she is passionate about photography, gardening, playing chess, and art. She loves psychology, history and journalism. She has been a Co-Author of more than 100 anthologies.

MY COUNTRY MY PEOPLE

A Country that is known to everyone,

Beautiful land filled with tall mountains,

Green Lands,

Magnificent Rivers,

Wide Various Cultures and Tradition,

Numerous Languages,

Unity In Diversity,

Land Of Great Heroes,

Martyred Warriors fought widely for Independence,

Divided by States And Union Territories,

Yet United by Various Things.

Our country has people,

With warm blood of fighting ability,

The blood that respects and cries for their soldiers,

The one's filled with harmony,

Among vivid Cultures,

I'm proud of my country people,

For their tolerating power,

But it's not needed anymore,

It's time to rebel against coups.

Our country is a great soil with the ideal thoughts of many,

Freedom fighters who shed their blood,

With deep patriotism in their hearts,

It is a country that fought with the Mughals, British and other invaders,

It is a country of democratic principles that other countries are inspired of,

My country is a great place with the most thrilling battle for freedom,

My Country My Pride.

3. KUMARI GUDIYA GAUTAM

नाम :कुमारी गुड़िया गौतम

शिक्षा :MA,ATD

पुरस्कार :२०० से ज्यादा प्राप्त है

प्रकाशित रचनाएं:३००से ज्यादा प्रकाशित हैं

गजल

देश का सैनिक देश की शान है,

जिसकी बस्ती देश ही में जान है।

जिससे देश में अमन शांति चैन है,

जिसके दिल में सिर्फ हिंदुस्तान है

हिन्दू- मुस्लिम आपस में न लड़ें ,

देश के सैनिक का ये अरमान है।

पैसे के लिए जीते और मरते लोग,

खुद का बेच रहे अब ईमान है।

बारिश हो या धूप या फिर ठंड,

करते हैं रक्षा देश की पहचान है।

देखो करो तुम अब नीत फौजीयो,

का अब आदर और सम्मान है।

भारत माता के सच्चे ये लाल है ,

जिसके लिए होते ये बलिदान है।

हर स्थिति में कर्म करें ये महान है,

जितना करें इनका कम बखान है।

देश के लिए हो जाएं शहिद तो,

सब देखो कैसे करते गुनणान है।

धारती में जन्मा ये पर हम सब,

के लिए मानो अब भगवान है।

4. NILOFAR FAROOQUI TAUSEEF

Nilofar Farooqui Tauseef, hails from Bihar Sharif, Nalanda but staying in Mumbai. She has done MCA & MBA. Team Leader by profession and writer by passion. She loves penning down her thoughts, emotions in her writing. For her "Pen is a sword to bring revolution". Her articles and research papers have been published in more than 300 books and magazines and in reputed journals of the country too. You can check her fb and instagram handled on-
@writernilofar

आज़ादी

अंग्रेज़ों की बेड़ियों को तोड़ आये हम।

पर गन्दे विचारों पर कौन लगाए मरहम?

न घटता है बलात्कार,

न कम होता है अत्याचार।

नज़रें घुमाकर देखो,

दिखता है हाहाकर, दिखता है हाहाकार।

छोटे कपड़े गर है बेकार,

बच्चियाँ क्यों होती है शिकार?

मुहब्बत करने वाला आखिर,

क्यों हो जाता है तड़ीपार?

आज़ादी का मतलब बस इतना सा है।

बदलो अपना विचार , बदलो अपना विचार।

दहेज की लालच में,

बेटी पे होता है अत्याचार।

किसान के बच्चे भूखे मरते,

या खुद कर लेता है तिरस्कार।

वीर सपूत जो जान गवाये, करते पहरेदार।

पेंशन की खातिर दर-दर भटके, उनका परिवार।

आज़ादी का मतलब बस इतना सा है।

बदलो अपना ये विचार , बदलो अपना ये विचार।

5. KAVITA VIJAYWARGIYA

कविता विजयवर्गीय मध्यप्रदेश के गुना से संबंध रखती हैं। उन्हें सिंगिंग करना , लिखना , पढ़ना , बच्चों के साथ मस्ती करना ये सब बेहद पसंद है। धर्म से जुड़ी हर चीज , हर बात उन्हें आकर्षित करती है।

आज़ाद भारत

हां हम आज़ाद हैं

इस आज़ादी का खुब लुत्फ उठाओ ,

जश्न मनाओ !

लेकिन....

कभी अपनी स्वतंत्रता ,

या आज़ादी का

ग़लत फायदा मत उठाओ !

हमें बोलने की आज़ादी मिली है

इसका अर्थ ये कदापि नही है

कि ,

किसी से बात करते वक्त कुछ भी बोल जाएं

शब्दों की मर्यादा को रख ताक पर

हम अपने मान सम्मान की बलि चढ़ाएं !!

6. BHAVNA MOHAN VIDHANI

सौ. भावना मोहन विधानी को लेखन के साथ-साथ गायन कुकिंग बागवानी भ्रमण और सामाजिक कार्यों का बहुत शौक है भावना जी ने 5 वर्षों तक सहायक शिक्षिका के रूप में भी कार्य किया है। भावना जी की कविताएं लेख लघु कथाएं कहानियां विभिन्न प्रकार की पत्र-पत्रिकाओं में प्रकाशित होती रहती हैं।

" मेरा स्वतंत्र भारत देश"

सर्वधर्म समभाव की संस्कृति वाला मेरा भारत देश सब देशों से महान और एक अद्भुत देश है, जहां हर धर्म के लोग मिलजुल कर एक साथ रहते हैं। सभी धर्मों को भारत देश में मान्यता है सब लोग अपने धर्म के अनुसार पूजा पाठ और त्योहार मना सकते हैं। मेरा भारत देश एक लोकतांत्रिक देश है जहां लोग मतदान कर अपनी इच्छा से सरकार बनाते हैं।

मेरे भारत देश की छटा सबसे निराली है, ऊंचे ऊंचे पर्वत चारो और बिखरी हरियाली, मन को मोह लेती है। मेरे भारत देश में अमीर हो या गरीब ऊंची जाति का हो या नीची जाति का सभी लोगों को एक समान अधिकार दिए गए हैं। मेरे भारत देश पर जब भी कोई मुसीबत आती है तो सरकार के साथ-साथ जनता भी कंधे से कंधा मिलाकर उस मुसीबत से बाहर निकालने का रास्ता निकालती है। मेरे भारत देश में भिन्न-भिन्न ने धर्म के लोग अपनी जाति के अनुसार पहनावे का चयन करते हैं। मेरे भारत देश में पुरानी संस्कृति के साथ साथ आधुनिक सोच और आधुनिक उपकरणों का भी उपयोग किया जाता है। मेरा भारत देश अपनी संस्कृति को भी साथ ले चलता है और वैज्ञानिक युग में नहीं सोच को अपनाकर विकास की और भी बढ़ता है। मेरे भारत देश की महान सेना हर पल अपने देशवासियों की सेवा में तत्पर रहती है। मैं दिल से अपने देश के प्रति कृतज्ञ हूं कि मैंने भारत जैसे महान देश में जन्म लिया है। और मैं हमेशा दिल से प्रार्थना करूंगी कि अपने देश के प्रति अपनी सारी जिम्मेदारियों और कर्तव्यों का पालन पूर्ण निष्ठा के साथ करूं। मैं परम पिता परमेश्वर से हमेशा प्रार्थना करूंगी कि मुझे जब भी जन्म मिले भारत देश में ही मिले। मेरे देश भारत की पावन भूमि को मेरा कोटि-कोटि प्रणाम।

सौ, भावना मोहन विधानी✍?

@bhavnavidhani123

7. HUNAR

She is Hunar a girl who believes in chasing the dreams.She loves to do public speaking and thus participates in many competitions and activities.She loves to explore the world that's why she like to travel listen songs and reading books.
She is a hodophile and musicophile.

INDEPENDENCE DAY

Independence Day is the most significant day in the history of Indian because it reminds us of the bravery and struggle of our freedom fighters. On this day we pay homage to our fighters who fought and gave up their lives for our independence. Since then we are celebrating our Independence Day every year on 15th August. It is considered a national holiday and all the organisations and institutions hoist the national flag and organise cultural functions across the country.

This day is celebrated to ignite the feeling of nationalism and patriotism across the country. Every citizen has a different viewpoint of Independence. A youngster takes this day to celebrate the glory and strength of the country while for others it's a reminder of the long suppression and cruelty that our people suffered. It's not only a celebration of Independence but also of unity with the diverse culture of the country.For about two centuries the Britishers managed to rule over us. Also, the resident of the nation endured a lot because of these oppressors. British authorities deal with us like slaves until we figure out how to retaliate against them.

We battled for our freedom yet work vigorously and magnanimously under the direction of our pioneers Jawahar Lal Nehru, Subhash Chandra Bose, Mahatma Gandhi,

Chandra Shekhar Azad, and Bhagat Singh. A portion of these pioneers picks the way of violence while some pick non-violence. The definitive point of these was to drive out the Britishers from the nation. Furthermore, on the fifteenth August 1947, the hotly anticipated dream works out as expected.

8. ANUSHKA DEEPAK JERE

A 15-year old reader from Mumbai, Maharashtra
chasing her
Dreams at its limit. Her heart cries to read and is
passionate
About writing poems. She believes "Where there's a
will there's
A way.. If there's no way, we can surely make our
own way..
God's grace!!"
You can reach her on Instagram @mee.anushkaa

INDIA,MY PRIDE !

The valleys of kindness,

The mountains of greatfulness,

The creation of God,

The story of Lord!

The peaks of intelligence,

The love of Almighty,

The sincerities of flora,

The formalities of fauna!

All can be seen,

Only where all the religions meet,

Only where full neighborhood dines together,

Only where brotherhood shines along like the peacock's
feather!

A stout little boy answered,

"It's the land of a golden bird

Which is free to roam from its nest

Oh, Oh yes, India!

Where Mahatma Gandhi took birth,

Where lies the great statue of Sardaar Vallabbhai Patel,

Where stands woman power curtailing man strength,

It's a strong word 'INDIA'

Where unity of India is a topic never to lose,

Where republic India pushed the British policy of Divide and Rule,

And the country stands again on its feet

With a new name 'Free India'!

It is indeed my pride to say,

"I am Anushka,

I am an Indian.

And India is my nationality..!"

9. LAVENYA

She is Lavenya from karnal, Haryana,born on 31 March 2006 - daughter of Mr.Rajinder Kumar and Mrs.Himali Manik. Her age is 16 years and her rudimentary avocations are listening songs, studying especially science , making reels and writing.

THE INDEPENDENCE

India,land of great people,

Filled with resources,

And national integrity.

Land of people,

Land of unity.

Land of prosperity,

Land of love.

Land on which martyr's died,

Land which gave birth to brave men,

Land on which I can die,

Land of which I am di-hearted fan.

The day of independence,

Huge day for Indians it meant,

Got freedom from people,

But chains of injustice are still left.

It's proud to be an indian,

Love to be an indian,

I love my country,

Now and forever.

10. RANBIR BHAKAT

Author by heart and passion. Writing since He was 16. Wrote about 700+ Anthologies & 2 Solo Book in preparation.

Gmail: ranbirbhakat5456@gmail.com

Insta Id: @_writing__tales_

BREATHE THE FREEDOM

Our's is a land of sages,

Known for bravery for ages.

None can with it compete,

Its culture none can beat.

Whatever caste or religion,

All live here in unison.

With rivers, sweet fountains,

It's a land of high mountains.

Its green forests are pretty,

And are source of prosperity.

Let's for it work hard,

For its safety, be on guard.

11. JAWAHAR B LALLA

Mr Jawahar B Lalla had been an accomplished senior management executive, writer, blogger, speaker, panel judge, and book reviewer having more than 40 + years of rich and vast IT technology experience.

INDEPENDENCE DAY

As I am penning my thoughts on Independence India.

My question to all is whether we are Independent as I still read news on women being molested & raped every day. I see politicians making a mockery of our law systems. I see doctors making money out of their professionals. Lawyers & Police are amending & reprimanding their rules on common citizens as per their preference.

Is there anybody for understands the grievances of common citizens of India?

I would like to see my country India as independent in the following ways.

First & Foremost it's my privilege to announce I am a proud citizen of India. Which has such a prosperous inheritance of Indian divinities, temples, Upanishads, Vedas & mythology epics to present globally. Going forward, I wish my Independent India to be among the top three countries in the world. I wish to witness courts, police & doctors performing their respective duties with complete sincerity & honesty. I wish poverty, slavery, sickness, prostitution, and corruption eradicated from my futuristic India. I wish every citizen of India to get their rights irrespective of caste in futuristic India. I wish all citizens of futuristic India to get the best of the best advanced medical treatments in super-built advanced hospitals built in our country with every child of India to have the best education system in futuristic India. I expect Indian roads, highways, connectivity of ports, and logistics transportation of cars, trains & air journeys to be the best internationally. I wish independent India to be so powerful & self-independent that we should be able to assist other countries instead of asking for their support. I wish our independent Indian currency to be one of the dominant currencies in the international forex money market yes now it has happened for international trade using Vistro account over swift transactions. I wish the government currency chest to hold the highest gold & forex reserves. I wish my independent India to implement strict laws against people who do money laundering & create black money for themselves. I wish every household in independent India to have roadways, highways, and logistics connections to various ports &airports .

Toilets, electricity & gas supply in each & every household. I wish independent India to have no slums It was said India was a golden country in which foreigners came & robbed us. I want to see independent India back as the golden country once more.

By ©Jawahar Lalla.

12. KAJARI GUHA

A published author who has authored several books
for the benefit of the students ...and one memoir
Bridging the gap---Shatarupa published by Partridge
Publishers
Composer of several songs ...
Writing is her goal but ..Music is her soul!
Presently won accolades for writing poetry in English
Bengali and Hindi.

गौरव गाथा

छवि प्यारी सी थी ..न वो थी कोई कल्पना !

युगों से भा रही थी वह तृप्त संस्कृति की अल्पना !

पूर्व पश्चिम उत्तर दक्षिण

सभी दिशाओं में था चमत्कार!

एक डाली पे खिले हुये थे

भारतमाता के पुष्प हज़ार!

वेद पुराण भगवदगीता से

झलके विद्वानों की कीर्ति!

पूरे विश्व को विह्वल करे

भारत की महिमा और प्रीति!

गौतम बुद्ध और विवेकानंद

थे भारतमाता के शांतिदूत!

बापू गांधी नेता सुभाष ने

झेला स्वतंत्रता की धूप!

ज्ञान विज्ञान से ओतप्रोत आर्यभट्ट

ने किया गणित का मान!

टैगोर और प्रेम चंद ने दिया

साहित्य को अचूक सम्मान!

वाल्मीकि ने रचा रामायण

किया विश्व में यह ऐलान!

श्रीराम और सीतामैया ने

मिलकर बसाया ये पुण्य धाम!

भारत की यह गौरव गाथा

सदा ही रहे शानदार!

आओ सभी अब मिलकर

झूमे गायें खुशी के गीत हज़ार!

©काजरी गुहा

13. USHA KALE

This is Usha Kale. This is 1st anthology . She have written few write ups on unique theme and topics. She's hailing from Shimoga. The way she write is simple and heart felt.

OUR INDIAN INDEPENDENCE

We all know that India got Independence on 15th August of 1947th year. Each and every citizen who belongs to India have to be proud and privileged to get the Independence from the British governance. The struggle behind the Independence is just indescribable. Each heroes and every freedom fighters played a crucial role as we all know but the blood stain and the family sentiment and emotion was not a thing infront of Independence. Women and kids too struggled very hard and leaded to bleed like anything. But our heroes never gave up and the courage and potential which Indians have is enormous and incompatible. To take stand and face the enemies is nothing like to between life ad death and yes our heroes and fighters never worried about life and death just thought and Independence (Aazaadhi) was the only word which was hearing all over India in the final moment and at last we got the Independence after loosing so many great heroes of India and we need to be grateful and sell gratitude to their feets with whole heart. Jai hind Bharath Matha ki jai ho.

14. KAMINI PRADHAN

कामिनी प्रधान, पिता- श्री मंगल प्रसाद प्रधान, माता -श्रीमती तपोवन्ती प्रधान , जो ग्राम पंचायत- आमगांव, शाखा -तमनार ,जिला -रायगढ़ छत्तीसगढ़ से रहने वाली है, जो अभी एम. एस .सी रसायन शास्त्र में अध्ययनरत है, जो पढ़ने, लिखने के साथ संगीत में रुचि रखती हैं।

स्वतंत्रता

स्वतंत्र भारत हुए टाइम हो गया लेकिन क्या आज भारत की बेटियां
स्वतंत्र है ...नहीं,

क्या करेंगे हम ऐसी स्वतंत्रता का जहां नारी के सम्मान के नाम पे
ढकोसले होते है ,

बाहर से लोग अच्छाई का दिखावा करते ,अंदर मन के सैतान को पनाह
देते है ,

अगर इसी तरह के भ्रष्टाचार बढ़ते रहे तो भारत स्वंत्र कैसे होगा ,

ना मारने के निसान , ना ही कोई पीड़ा दिखती नारिया भी कमाल है
चुप चाप अपने दर्द सह जाती ,

इतने पीड़ा को देखते हुए भी लोगो के सामने खुश रहने का अच्छा
मजाक कर लेती है ,

स्वतंत्र कहा हुई नारिया अब भी लोगो के दबाव में अपनी जिंदगी जी
रही है ,

हाल पूछने वाला कोई नहीं , पल भर के लिए समझने वाला कोई नहीं ,

तब भी चुप रहती है उंगली नही उठाती लोगो पर ,

क्या यह सही है नहीं ... बिल्कुल भी नहीं ..

दबी आवाज़ को जुबां तक लाने की हिम्मत देनी होगी हमे ,

उनके लिए खड़े होने के लिए अब भी अच्छाई जिंदाहाई ,

डरना नहीं है उन्हें हाथ थामकर उनका साथ देना होगा ,

वो खड़ी होंगी अपने लिए ,अपने अधिकारों के लिए ,

तब जाकर भारत पूरी तरह स्वंत्रा होगा , स्वंत्रता के गीत गाएगा ।

15. CHESTA SINGH LAKHAWA

Chesta Singh Lakhhawat is a grade XII biology student. She's interested in writing on real-life incidents. She sees every challenging situation in life as a race which has to be won.

INDIAN TRICOLOUR

It's being rightly said that the Indian tricolor is not flying just because the wind is blowing it but it's flying due to the last breath of every soldier who died protecting it. Independence is not a word It's a process which took the sacrifices of millions of Indian people before and after independence to bring India to its level. Mahatma Gandhi did play a critical role in Indian Independence but we can't ignore the sacrifices of shaheed Bhagat Singh, Chandrashekhar Azad,Jhansi Ki Rani and many more..... we didn't got independence just by the non cooperation movement or civil disobedience movement started by Mahatma Gandhi but it took the it took the lives of millions of Indian soldiers and Indian people who struggled to fight against the British rule even a person who couldn't arrange the two times meal for his family fought against the Britishers by seeing the courageous people like Bhagat Singh and Pratap Singh Ji Barot who died at the age of 21 years we don't know anything about the people like Pratap Singh Ji Barrett because he belong to Akash whose population is very very less. Mothers did encouraged that children to join the army and fight against the British at an early age of 17 years. And now after independence India is again picking up speed and trying to gain the same importance which it had before the British encountered India so at the end I would just like to say

" कदम बढ़ा चला है यह देश अपनी गणतंत्रता कि ओर....

होगा यह विश्व नायक चारो दिशाओं मे है यही शोर....

दुशमन चाहे करले अपनी कोशिश पुरज़ोर....

अब तो न रुकेगा और लाएगा विश्व मे एक नई भोर.....”

16. JAI GOPAL ARORA

He is Jai Gopal, a young writer from New Delhi, who started writing in lockdown for timepass. But, now he wanna become a professional writer. His poems has been published in no. Of anthologies. He writes in Hindi but also have a deep interest in Sanskrit. He study Vedas, Upnishads and Puranas. He also study Bhagvad geeta.

स्वतंत्रता के स्वतंत्रता सेनानी

विसर्जित हो गए चिताओं पर, स्वतंत्रता सैनानी हमारे,

ना जाने कितने घाव झेले, ना जाने कितने शत्रु मारे ?

बली चढ़ गए स्वतंत्रता की, चिता बनाई शय्या।

चूम लिया अंगारों को, चुन गए दिवारों में,

फांसी पर झूल लिए, अमर हो गए कृपाणों के वारों से।

अर्श में तारा बन चमक उठे, बन गए शहादत का अलंकार,

फिरंगियों के लिए बन गए वो मौत का अवतार।

मृत्यु को प्राप्त हो, अंकित कर गए तिरंगे पर अपने खून के दाग,

करे आंदोलन, जीते संग्राम, करा उन वीरों महाविरों ने मृत्यु से अनुराग।

बोल इनकलाब जिंदाबान, रण में हो गए लहू लूहान,

लड़े अंतिम श्वास तक एसे वो बलवान।

क्या उनके ऋण से कभी उरिन हो पाएगा यह देश?

प्राण गवां कर स्वतंत्रता दी, धर मृत्यु का वेश।

17. ANKITA NAHAR

#AKII#@@@ अंकिता नाहर मूल रूप से अजमेर, राजस्थान की रहने वाली हैं। ये लिखने के लिए हमेशा उत्साहित रहती है साथ ही हमेशा शब्दों से सुकून सा पाती हैं। ये अपने विचारों और जो भी इन्होंने अपनी जिंदगी से सीखा है, अनुभव लिया है उसे अपनी रचनाओं में लिख देती हैं। इससे इनकी रचनाएँ बहुत ही ज्यादा भावुक भावों वाली और प्रभावशाली बन जाती हैं। जो कि पढ़ने वालों को बहुत आकर्षित करती है। वह इस माध्यम को और आगे तक ले जाना चाहती हैं। आप इनकी रचनाओं को इंस्टाग्राम @naharankita1 पर पढ़ सकते हैं।

स्वतंत्रता दिवस

सुना हैं अच्छी चीजो को बनने ने समय लगता है

वैसे ही समय लगा था भारत के संविधान में

समय लगा था भारत की आजादी में

समय लगा था भारत को भारत बनने में

और ना जाने क्या क्या लगा था

१५ अगस्त को स्वतंत्रता दिवस बनने में

ना जानें कितने लोग वीरगति को प्राप्त हुए

ना जाने कितनो के सिंदूर और कितनी माओं की कोख़ आजादी में काम
आयी

आज भी याद हैं मुझे

मां अक्सर सुनाया करती हैं

भगतसिंह का बलिदान,

पद्मावती का जौहर

शिवाजी, रानी लक्ष्मीबाई

और ना जाने कितने ही वीरों

की कहानियां

मैं बात करूं उन वीरांगनओं की

इतने शब्द मेरे पास हैं नहीं

बस इतना ही कहूंगी की

मौत तुझसे बहुत ज्यादा सिफारिश नहीं हैं

बस जब भी तू आए

तब ऐसी आये की

सिर पर कफ़न नहीं तिरंगा हो ।

©AKII #@@@

18. B RAJ KUJMAR

B Raj Kumar an electrical engineer by qualification has 35 years of work experience spanning various industries. He wants to pursue his passion of writing poetry and novels in English as his 2nd career.

ARE WE FREE ?

I am not sure if we are liberated,

I am either berated or derated.

In a world filled up with envy and contempt,

Is it not I am tech savvy and do attempt?

I freed up from each negative thought,

I wanted to be picked up from lucky lot.

I started believing that all is in the mind,

I did not want my shackles to remind.

There is a price to pay for freedom,

That reminds to discontinue one's fiefdom.

True liberty comes with acceptance of all,

That ensures you lift up even those who fall.

19. ROOPAL ARORA

She is Roopal Arora.She has done BE in IT.She has done MBA in IT.She is OCP and SAP professional.She is a brainmaths professional.She has 6 years experience in Wipro and CNEB as IT professional.She is remotely working for Marucom as Manager Technical.

INDIAN INDEPENDENCE

India is a land of diversity where people of different castes,cultures,religions and beliefs live together.The Independence Day reminds every Indian of the beginning of a new life free from bondage.It was with constant and determined years of efforts of freedom fighters that India got its independence.It is celebrated throughout India with big ceremonies including National Flag hoisting,speeches,skits,songs,dances,competitions on different freedom fighters and various movements.It unites diverse individuals all over the country.

The leaders give speech about struggles and achievements of our political leaders.The Independence Day Fair follows next.This is collection of events and showcase of cultures,traditions of different states of India.It is celebrated with happiness and excitement.All leaders and people gather in large numbers to see the Independence day parade.

Tributes are paid to the freedom fighters.It is observed with great honour at all schools,colleges and offices.Some historical buildings are decorated beautifully.Sweets are distributed among everyone.We feel elated and it motivates us to protect our country against its enemies.We should learn from our freedom fighters and try to make our country great.The day lets us to rejoice in spirit of freedom.We remember great sacrifices of our leaders.Independence is the freedom of soul,perception of mind and understanding of heart.It celebrates our nation's freedom after struggle and sacrifice.It is celebration of our country's diverse cultures.It inspires us to stay united and happy with each other.

20. JOHANA MIRACLINE SS

Pursuing master's degree in English language, love to explore the world Everyone probably thinks that they are the best because poets teach you to think about everything in a new way, about yourself or the world. Poets have a lot of things going on.

INDEPENDENCE DAY

It's a victory after a long process

The ability to rule is learnt lately

They withstand inner confidence and motivation

And a outrage to be self independent to held up high

The little spark of self realisation and fame

That fire ups each other and uproot for themselves

Sovereignty of the liberty of the people

Freedom a footnote of self legislation adminstration.

21. HUMA MALIK

She is Huma Malik who hails from a small town of Dehradun which is encompassed by alluring blue valleys. She is a student of College of Vocational Studies, University of Delhi. She is obsessed with writing and penning down her heart out with great zeal and enthusiasm to regale the joy of life.

INDEPENDENCE DAY

I glanced London, Paris and Japan …

No corner of the world has another Hindustan.

India , Bhaarat, Hindustaan whatsoever this pious holy land is known as but the people of India call it the BHAARAT MATA. The land which holds the blood of a lot of legendaries in its wharfage, the perspiration of a lot of farmers who irrigate this land with their sweat, the mothers who sacrificed their sons so that the lineage could sustain freely. This is what OUR WATAN HINDUSTAAN known for!!!

India is a land of distinct culture which is thrived by distinct religions, languages, cuisines, dresss and tribal communities. The country serves its people with the whole heart. No one is being discriminated on the basis of colour, caste, creed, religion and language. In order to maintain the equality and peace in the country , the constitution does not confer on one particular National language for the country. English is considered as the official language of India. India's preamble conspicuously defines the sovereignty where the state would not intervene in the religious matters. The country is free to adopt any code of dress to be worn by the men and women of particular domain. No restrictions are being imposed on the type of food one can consume. All in all India is a territory where people live by their heart not by the imposition of their ruler. It is a union of 28 states and 9 union territories which makes a conglomeration of largest galaxies of fraternity, brotherhood, equality and beauty in the hearts of Indians.

India welcomes its guests and considers them the incarnation of GOD and their warm welcome lead them to live their rest of the life on this pious land of lords. History has witnessed a good many examples of welcoming the foreigners and leading them to be a part of this land.

Notwithstanding the other nations have conquered the colossal distant lands however India has conquered the HEARTS of all the distant PEOPLE.

THIS IS THE BEAUTY OF OUR MOTHERLAND - INDIA & IT'S PEOPLE.

22. SANGEETA KUMARI

Sangeeta Kumari,She is a faculty of Political Science.She loves to write poems and stories.

INDEPENDENCE DAY

75th Independence Day

This is our 75th Independence Day.On 15 August 1947, India became independent from the British Empire.On this day, the nation's Prime Minister hoisted the tricolour at Red Fort to mark India's independence from the British Imperial Crown.

Mahatma Gandhi had started freedom fight in India, also launched and directed three major campaigns in the Indian Independence Movement,which are Non-cooperation in 1919-1922,The Civil Disobedience Movement and The Salt Satyagraha of 1930-193,and the Quit India Movement from about 1940-1942. Mahatma Gandhi is also known as the Father Of The Nation.

Sarojini Naidu is known as the Mother Of The Nation in Jai Hind or Vande Matram is the most popular slogan in our India,whose origins in the movement for Indian independence.Indian Mutiny, also called Sepoy Mutiny or First War of Independence were started the Indian independence movement in 1857.Dr.Bhim Rao Ambedkar is known as the father of the Indian Constitution.

Pingali Venkayya were designed Indian flag in 1947.There are three colours in the national flag....

The Saffron colour indicates strength and courage of the country.

The white colour indicates peace and truth.

The green colour shows the fertility, growth and auspiciousness of the land.

Ashoka Chakra means, It represents the dynamism of a peaceful change.

23. SHEKH MAZIDA KHATUN

She makes her identity by herself. She was an IT Sector Student. A Prolific Writer On Yourquote App. She was a Compiler of 2 books. She was also An Author. She left her marks on published 35+ books.

स्वतंत्रता दिवस

वतन से मोहब्बत सिर्फ़ एक दिन नहीं,

उम्र भर दिल में बनाए रखना।

फौजी की तरह वतन के लिए मिटने,

सदेव त्यार रहना।

सिर्फ़ स्वतंत्र दिवस ही न दे सलामी देश को और जवानों को,

इज्ज़त एक फौजी की 365 दिन हर लम्हें करना।

सुकून दो पल परिवार के संग गुजारना उनके क़िस्मत में नहीं,

मगर अपने परिवार को छोड़ जो देश के लिए निकले,

उन्हें कैसे भूले कोई।

कहना बस इतना है

जो सीना रखते हैं फौजी,

वहीं सीना रखने की, कीजाए कोशिश पूरी।

24. MISS RITUPARNA DUTTA

इनका नाम रितुपर्णा है जो की आसाम शहर की निवासी है।

आजादी

आजादी की उस दौर में

ना जाने कितने हाथों ने

खोया अपनों का हाथ

कितने उबरती हुई सपनों ने

छोड़ा जिंदगी का साथ।

उस जज़्बे में उमंग था

जिसने हज़ारों दिलों में

देश भक्ति का भाव जगाया,

आँखों में आजादी का सपना सजाया ।

तिरंगे को दिखने के लिए उठी नजरों ने

किसी और के आगे झुकना जरूरी ना समझा ।

यही तो वह वजह है जिसके कारण

आज हम आजादी मना पा रहे हैं।

यह आजादी देशप्रेमियों के बलिदान का फल हैं

जो आज हमें हमारी जान से भी प्यारी हैं ।।

@Rituparna Dutta

Instagram id-rituparna2098

25. C. MAHALAKSHMI

A passionate writer of simple words with deep meaning in it. First of all, words are the best medium to elaborate our feelings in life.

Finished teacher training and currently doing the masters in English literature. As a student of literature, there is a plenty of interest in writing review, short story, poem, criticism and quotes.

A housewife and also a mother with lot of dreams.

INDEPENDENCE DAY

India is a land of unity in diversity,

Independence is the primary key to abolish slavery,

Not only India, all the human in this world should be independent,

Independent India is the future of many unsung warriors in the freedom struggle,

Freedom doesn't meant to be a simple one,

It should be unique with all possible things that are lined up for the better tomorrow for an individual's Society,

Today is the last day of the slavery as well as the dependent on british people for all the things,

No more quarreling, no more struggling,

Just get what you want,

Freedom - equality, liberty, integrity and patriotic society,

Freedom for expressing the thoughts and ideas,

Freedom to do what you dream of,

Freedom to go wherever you want,

And finally, today is the independence day in the midnight
of this August,

Moments filled with goosebumps and honor walk with few
national leaders,

Jai hind.

(a broken poem of an unsung hero in the freedom struggle)

26. ANITA ROHLAN

अनिता रोहलन का जन्म नागौर के जिले लाछड़ी गाँव में हुआ यह
सबको सकारात्मक जीवन जीने की प्रेरणा है यह एम,ए की छात्रा
है
इनकी 100 पुस्तकों मे कविताएँ प्रकाशित हो चुकी है
इनकी पहली स्वरचित पुस्तक "सफर_ए_जिंदगी " है

लिखना है आज जरूरी

लिखना है आज जरूरी

विपदा जो बरस पड़ी है

जन-जन पर भारी

बेबस,लाचार,हो गये सब

शोहरत वाले भी धरा पे सो पड़े

हाथ जो न थामा अब एक दुसरे का

तबाह कर जायेगा यह पृथ्वी हमारी

प्रलयकार का अब वक्त है

पथ पे डटकर रहा है खड़े

वरना विस्फोटक की अग्नि भारी

जला देगी प्रकृति हमारी

इन घुसपेठियो को है हराना

मेरी देश की माटी को सै बचाना

,वायु,जल,थल,

सैना ने संभाली है कमान भारी

हर तरफ शोर है

भाईचारे का

हम है आजाद भारत के निवासी तो हर दिन

मर मिटेगे पर माँ धरती पर ना आँच आने देंगे

~आराध्यापरी

27. DR. MAJOR NALINI JANARDHANAN

Dr (Major) Nalini Janardhanan, is a doctor who served in Indian Army as an Army Medical Officer She is a popular writer of Kerala who got Katha Award and a writer of many medical books for which she got IMA Sahithya Award. She is an Akashvani(All India Radio) and Doordarshan approved artist of Ghazals and Bhajans.

UNITY

proud to see Feeling our tricolor

Swinging high in the sky.

The nature showing tricolor during

Sunset near green fields.

The national flag symbolizes for us

Patriotism, unity and sacrifice.

It is not just a colorful cloth for us

It fills our hearts with pride.

Remembering our soldiers who sacrifice

Family, comforts and lives.

The memorable words of Capt Batra,

"Either I will come back after hoisting the

Tricolor or I will come back wrapped in it."

We are united as Indians and

We love our nation, our glory.

Salutes to the men in uniform

Their service and martyrdom.

The great sons of Mother India,

We are proud of you always!

May the tricolor furl high in the sky

My nation, India is the best!

Dr Major Nalini Janardhanan

28. HENA NOOR AAIN

Her name is Hena Noor Aain
She live in Kolkata.She completed her graduation in
history honour .

THE INDEPENDENCE DAY

The independence is all about

a beauty of love which

express through eyes.

The independence is the

most precious day for everyone

Because that day is all about

a beauty of life which make your life beautiful.

29. AZAD ASHRAF MADRE

AZAD ASHARAF MADRE a Poet from Chiplun,Maharashtra. Father Of A Girl "SAKINA". Inspiration of writing "SAIMA". Loves to writes poems of love, Social Awareness and Issues of Common Man. His Poem's Published in anthologies like "Ruh e Mohabbat" and Shrihind Publication's Anthology "Flames Of My Imagination".

मेरा वतन

कितना प्यारा है मेरा प्यारा वतन,

दुनिया में न्यारा मेरा न्यारा वतन।

कहीं भी जाओ अच्छा नही लगता,

कितना अच्छा है ये हमारा वतन।

कुर्बानियां इसकी मिट्टी में शामिल,

सबको है जान से ये प्यारा वतन।

आज़ादी तब जाकर मिली हमको,

जब भी एक के होकर लड़ा है वतन।

आज़ाद कुर्बान इसकी अज़मत पे,

है हरएक आंख का जो तारा वतन।

30. VAISHNAVI PURANIK

She Vaishnavi Puranik. Town Kumbhasi Kundapur
Taluk Udupi District.
Her Father name is Lakshminarayan Puranik Mother's
name is Radha Puranik.
Education: MA economics.
DCA on Computer. RA and PGDCA.
Especially CLT *First Rank Pass*

Cheluve

<u>Amrita_Bharatige_Kannadadarati</u>

Kannada's debt is irredeemable

Diversity does not obscure unity

The taste of honey butter is irresistible

The service of Bharatamma is not over

We must say that we are all the same

Worship should be done holding a pious stanza

Everyone should serve Kannada

We have to be born again as soldiers

As a farmer you have to sow the seed in the land

Porridge should be eaten in the house of the poor

One should hold the pen as a great achiever

The blood of the enemy should be offered like Obavva

Floors of art must be cast

The aroma of culture and arts should be spread

It should be cultivated as the karmabhoomi of the achievers

A place of culture should be permanent

Amrita_Bharatige_Kannadadarati

You are devoted to us

Aarti should be lit for the soldiers

We have to bring the strength ourselves

Vaishnavi Puranic Udupi